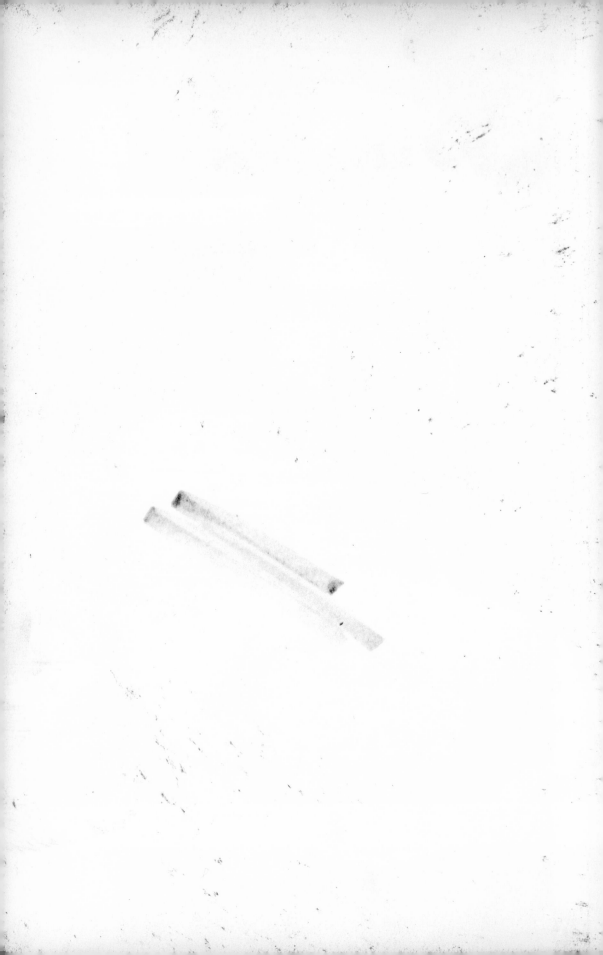

Visual Geography Series®

MOROCCO

...in Pictures

Prepared by
Geography Department

Lerner Publications Company
Minneapolis

Photo by Maryknoll Missioners

**Surrounded by her children, this woman fashions a rug to
sell at one of Morocco's many outdoor markets.**

This book is an all-new edition in the Visual Geography Series. Previous editions were published by
Sterling Publishing Company, New York City. The
text, set in 10/12 Century Textbook, is fully revised
and updated, and new photographs, maps, charts, and
captions have been added.

LIBRARY OF CONGRESS CATALOGING-IN-PUBLICATION DATA

Morocco in pictures / prepared by Geography
  Department, Lerner Publications Company.
    p. cm. — (Visual geography series)
    Rev. ed. of: Morocco in pictures / prepared by Noel
  Sheridan.
    Includes index.
    Summary: An introduction to the geography, his-
  tory, government, economy, culture, and people of
  the north African country that is ten miles away from
  Spain.
    ISBN 0-8225-1843-0 (lib. bdg.)
    1. Morocco. [1. Morocco.] I. Sheridan, Noel. Mo-
  rocco in pictures. II. Lerner Publications Company.
  Geography Dept. III. Series: Visual geography series
  (Minneapolis, Minn.)
  DT305.M65 1989   88-9126
  964—dc19   CIP
                                                  AC

International Standard Book Number: 0-8225-1843-0
Library of Congress Catalog Card Number: 88-9126

VISUAL GEOGRAPHY SERIES®

Publisher
Harry Jonas Lerner
Associate Publisher
Nancy M. Campbell
Senior Editor
Mary M. Rodgers
Editor
Gretchen Bratvold
Assistant Editors
Philip E. Baruth
Dan Filbin
Kathleen S. Heidel
Illustrations Editor
Karen A. Sirvaitis
Consultants/Contributors
Isaac Eshel
Sandra K. Davis
Designer
Jim Simondet
Cartographer
Carol F. Barrett
Indexer
Sylvia Timian
Production Manager
Gary J. Hansen

Courtesy of United Nations

**A craftsperson stands beside his intricately designed wood
carving.**

Acknowledgments

Title page photo courtesy of Royal Air Maroc.

Elevation contours adapted from *The Times Atlas of
the World*, seventh comprehensive edition (New York:
Times Books, 1985).

2 3 4 5 6 7 8 9 10 98 97 96 95 94 93 92 91

A shepherd grazes his flock of sheep along a road south of Casablanca, a city on Morocco's western coast.

Contents

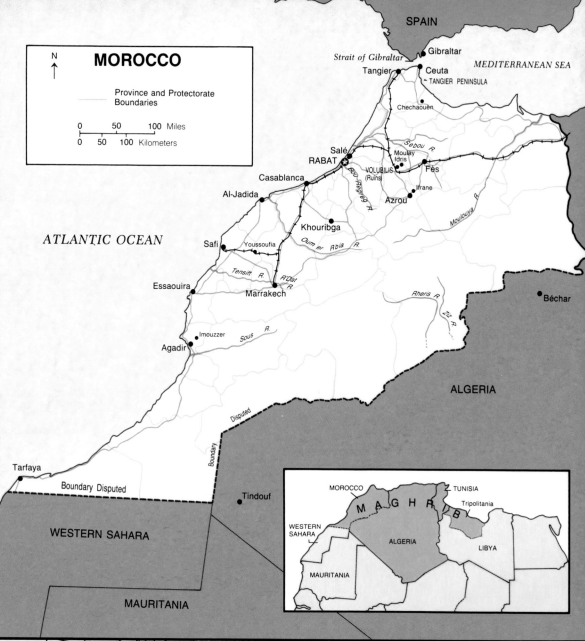

MOROCCO

N

Province and Protectorate Boundaries

0   50   100 Miles
0 50 100 Kilometers

SPAIN

Strait of Gibraltar Gibraltar

MEDITERRANEAN SEA

Tangier Ceuta
TANGIER PENINSULA

Chechaouèn

Sebou R.

Salé
RABAT Moulay Idris
VOLUBILIS (Ruins) Fès

Casablanca *Bou Regreg R.* Ifrane

Al-Jadida Azrou

Moulouya R.

ATLANTIC OCEAN

Khouribga

Safi Youssoufia *Oum er Rbia R.*

Tensift R. *R'Dat R.*

Essaouira *Rheris R.*

Marrakech *Ziz R.*

Béchar

Imouzzer *Sous R.*

Agadir

ALGERIA

Disputed

Boundary

Tarfaya

Boundary Disputed

Tindouf

WESTERN SAHARA

MOROCCO
TUNISIA
Tripolitania
M A G H R I B
WESTERN SAHARA
ALGERIA
LIBYA
MAURITANIA

MAURITANIA

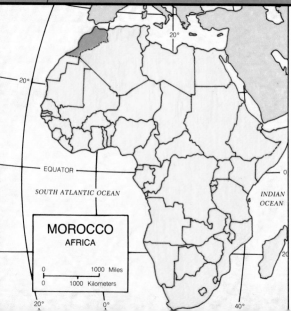

20°

20°

EQUATOR

SOUTH ATLANTIC OCEAN

INDIAN OCEAN

MOROCCO
AFRICA

0   1000 Miles
0   1000 Kilometers

20° 0° 40°

METRIC CONVERSION CHART
To Find Approximate Equivalents

WHEN YOU KNOW:	MULTIPLY BY:	TO FIND:
AREA		
acres	0.41	hectares
square miles	2.59	square kilometers
CAPACITY		
gallons	3.79	liters
LENGTH		
feet	30.48	centimeters
yards	0.91	meters
miles	1.61	kilometers
MASS (weight)		
pounds	0.45	kilograms
tons	0.91	metric tons
VOLUME		
cubic yards	0.77	cubic meters
TEMPERATURE		
degrees Fahrenheit	0.56 (*after* subtracting 32)	degrees Celsius

Horseshoe-shaped archways and geometrically patterned walls, such as those decorating this palace in Casablanca, typify Moroccan architecture. The building style is also referred to as Moorish—after the historical period beginning in the eighth century A.D., when Moroccan culture reflected the combined influences of Spanish and Arab traditions.

Introduction

Morocco lies within nine miles of Spain and has long been a bridge between Europe and the Arab-dominated countries of Africa. Historically, Morocco was known only as a small part of a vast African expanse called the Maghrib—an Arabic word meaning "the time or place of the sunset."

The Maghrib included present-day Morocco, Algeria, Tunisia, and northwestern Libya.

A mountain-dwelling people known as the Berbers have maintained their traditional lifestyle in Morocco's Atlas peaks for 4,000 years. Arabs, who first migrated

5

to the Maghrib in the seventh century are the only foreign group to take firm root on Moroccan soil. European powers governed for less than a century before returning Morocco to independent rule.

Since Morocco won its independence in 1956, it has seen both impressive technological development and serious social problems. The nation's communication and transportation networks are among the most advanced in North Africa. Yet overpopulation, poverty, drought, and large migrations from poor rural areas to crowded cities are still pressing issues.

King Hassan II, Morocco's ruler since 1961, is also the spiritual leader of the nation's huge majority of Muslims (followers of the Islamic religion). But radical student activists and Muslim fundamentalists—whose goal is to have the government function under Islamic law—have grown stronger each year since independence. Many students want power to be granted by election. Strict Muslims, however, support the king and feel that he must take a more aggressive stance in foreign policy. As a result of these conflicting tensions, several riots occurred in the 1980s.

Despite these internal troubles, Morocco has improved its relations with the Western Sahara, which lies to the southwest. Morocco long claimed the region based on 900-year-old boundaries. A small but effective military force called the Polisario opposed Morocco's claim, fighting a war for independence.

As of early 1991, the war was in a ceasefire. A peace plan sponsored by the United Nations appears to be leading to a negotiated settlement of the conflict, which has drained the Moroccan treasury for 15 years. Morocco's government and the Polisario's leaders have agreed on the terms of a public vote that will decide the future of the Western Sahara.

Traditional suqs, or markets, remain a vital part of Moroccan life.

From the low elevation of the R'Dat River Valley, the High Atlas Mountains stretch to the horizon in a series of irregular, heavily forested peaks.

1) The Land

Morocco lies in the northwestern corner of the African continent and has roughly 1,700 miles of shoreline. The Moroccan coast runs west along the Mediterranean Sea toward the Strait of Gibraltar before turning south to face the Atlantic Ocean. Ceuta, a city on Morocco's northern Tangier Peninsula, is located only nine miles away from Spain.

Algeria borders Morocco to the east, southeast, and south. Over 600 miles of this border, between the Algerian cities of Béchar and Tindouf, have been in dispute since 1963. To the south lies the Western Sahara (formerly known as the Spanish Sahara), a vast desert region that Morocco has occupied militarily since 1976. Not including this region, which most countries do not recognize as part of Morocco, the nation covers 174,000 square miles— an area that is slightly larger than the state of California.

Topography

High, rugged mountain ranges dominate Morocco's topography and divide the country into three major regions. To the west of the mountains lie the Atlantic coastal lowlands, which support most of the country's population and agriculture. The mountains themselves form the interior region, which includes fertile valleys wedged among the peaks. East of the high peaks is a semi-arid region called the pre-Sahara, where the mountains descend into high plateaus before fading into the Sahara Desert.

ATLANTIC COASTAL LOWLANDS

Bounded on the south by the westernmost High Atlas Mountains, Morocco's Atlantic coastal strip is flat and regular, interrupted occasionally by sand dunes or marshes. The majority of the country's population is located in the western region between the cities of Tangier and Essaouira. Elevations rarely exceed 1,500 feet above sea level. Two major plains—the Rharb in the north and the Doukkala to the south—have the richest soil in the country. An object of conquest for centuries, this area includes the important cities of Rabat and Casablanca.

East of the lowlands is a broad plateau that stands at the foothills of the mountains. Although barren, this plateau is rich

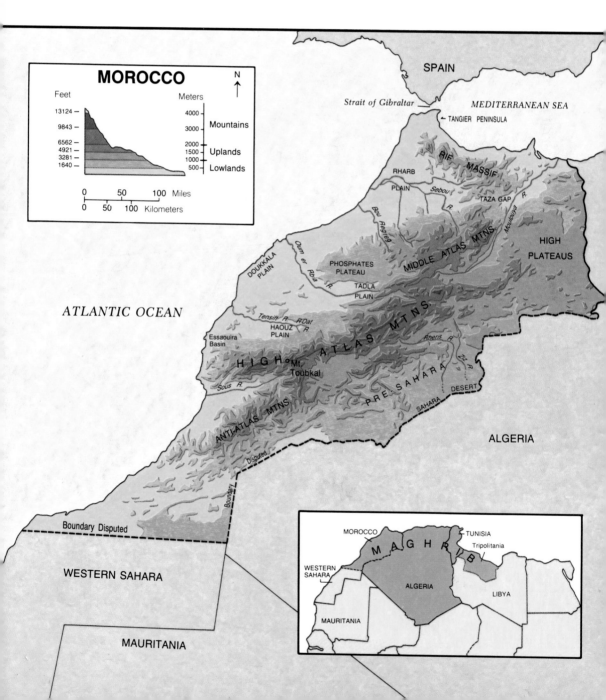

Mountain streams flow freely at Azrou, located east of the phosphates plateau.

in the phosphate rock from which it takes its name—the phosphates plateau. Two farmable plains—the Tadla and the Haouz —lie between the phosphates plateau and the mountains. The rivers flowing out of the Atlas ranges provide these regions with water and fertile topsoil.

INTERIOR MOUNTAINS

Although nearly all of the mountain ranges in the country extend from northeast to southwest, the Rif Massif (range) is confined to Morocco's northern region and runs parallel to the Mediterranean coast. These mountains seldom reach more than 7,000 feet above sea level. The Rif range drops steeply into the Mediterranean Sea and cuts off most of the country from the northern Tangier Peninsula.

Three sections of the Atlas Mountains form the major barrier between the At-

lantic Ocean and the Sahara Desert. Just south of the Rif are the Middle Atlas Mountains, which include both plateaus and peaks that rise from 4,000 to 10,000 feet above sea level. In ancient times, the only access from east to west in the area was through the narrow Taza Gap, an opening between the Rif and Middle Atlas ranges.

The second and third sections—the High Atlas Mountains and the Anti-Atlas Mountains—are tall and wide enough to produce a nationwide split in climate. The peaks prevent moisture-rich coastal winds from meeting the dry, easterly winds off the Sahara. The main stretch of the High Atlas Mountains has summits over 10,000 feet, and snow covers them most of the year. The most impressive peak is Toubkal (13,665 feet), the highest mountain in North Africa. The southern Anti-Atlas range closely borders the High Atlas, appearing in contrast as a group of very high hills.

HIGH PLATEAUS AND THE PRE-SAHARA

East of the Middle Atlas Mountains are the High Plateaus, which make up a uniformly level region about 3,500 feet above the sea. These plateaus, combined with the Taza Gap farther north, have traditionally formed an important communication and transportation route between Algeria and Morocco.

South of the High Plateaus and to the east of the High Atlas range lies the pre-Sahara. This region is composed of *hamaidiya*—rocky desert areas at elevations of 1,600 to 3,200 feet. In the pre-Sahara are occasional oases (fertile spots in the desert) that are watered by rivers from the Atlas Mountains. Sand dunes also begin in the region, representing the small portion of actual Sahara Desert enclosed within Morocco's official boundaries.

Independent Picture Service

Southern rivers often dry up under conditions of low rainfall and desert heat.

Rivers

Morocco's river system is the most extensive in North Africa, but none of the rivers are navigable. They have been dammed heavily to provide the country with water for irrigation as well as for hydroelectric power.

Rivers generally flow northwest down to the Atlantic Ocean and southeast down to the Sahara Desert. The chief exception is the Moulouya River, which travels northeast for 320 miles before emptying into the Mediterranean Sea. The Ziz and the Rheris are the two major waterways running into the Sahara. Upon reaching the semi-arid plateaus, these streams lose much of their force through evaporation and eventually dry up completely.

Five major rivers—the Sebou, Bou Regreg, Oum er Rbia, Tensift, and Sous—empty into the Atlantic. The Sebou and its tributaries provide 45 percent of the country's water resources. The Sebou's lower

Independent Picture Service

Giant sand dunes characterize the landscape in Morocco's Ziz River Valley.

10

Contrasting with the desert terrain are the snowy slopes of the Middle Atlas Mountains.

The mild climate of Rabat, the capital of Morocco, enables palm trees to thrive along a main street of the city.

section waters the prosperous Rharb farming region, and the government plans to build 13 dams on the river over a span of 25 years.

Climate

Morocco's interior mountains divide the country into two climatic regions. Moderate weather prevails near the sea, and hot conditions are common inland. In the north and west, winters are cool and wet, with plentiful rainfall. Summers in these regions are hot—despite brisk sea breezes in the afternoon—and dry, with little precipitation. The southwest, south, and southeast possess a desertlike climate that brings little rain, hot summers, and mild winters.

Rabat, the capital city, has pleasant temperatures averaging 62° F in winter and 82° F in summer. The city of Marrakech has temperatures that range from a low of 40° F in winter to a summer high of 101° F. In the High Atlas Mountains temperatures fall below zero in the winter, and summers are cool and pleasant, with occasional thunderstorms.

The mountain regions of Morocco receive large amounts of precipitation. Some of the moisture arrives in the form of snow, which remains on the peaks for up to nine months. The southern and eastern slopes, however, are generally dry. The Rif in the north receives roughly 40 inches of rain annually, while Marrakech and Rabat each receive less than 20 inches of rain per year.

Flora and Fauna

The Moroccan countryside features an unusual range of plant life. Among the more plentiful of the country's species is the dwarf palm, whose leaves are used to stuff mattresses; the asphodel, a lilylike plant with yellow or white spikes; and fennel, an herb of the carrot family. The western plateaus are covered with various grasses, such as esparto and alfa grass. Date palms survive in the desert, but only near oases.

In one year a single date palm tree may yield as much as 600 pounds of fruit.

The pattern and color of the feathers of the insect-eating scops owl are remarkably similar to those of tree bark.

Forests cover an estimated 15 million acres, or nearly 15 percent of the country's area. The thickest and most varied growth is found in the Middle Atlas Mountains, where evergreen oaks flourish. Morocco's forests were even more abundant before overgrazing and extensive woodcutting led to soil erosion in many areas. In addition, the tanning industry stripped vast stands of green and cork oaks of their bark. Trees are still plentiful, however. With government protection, native cedar and pine as well as imported eucalyptus now thrive.

Wild boars are found in all mountain regions, but they inhabit primarily the western High Atlas and Middle Atlas mountains. Jackals, rabbits, porcupines, and hedgehogs are still abundant. Striped hyenas can be found in the dry eastern sections, and mountain cats roam the Atlas Mountains. In the Rif, hunters use ferrets (weasel-like mammals) to chase rabbits. The mountains are also full of birdlife, including hawks, eagles, and owls. Doves and partridges are common throughout the country. Poisonous snakes—such as vipers, puff adders, and cobras—live primarily in the south.

The slender-billed, richly shaded bee eater nests as far south as Australia and as far east as Asia. This type — *Merops apiaster* — can be seen in Morocco and in southern Europe.

Courtesy of Chris Loggers

Courtesy of Chris Loggers

The tail-less Barbary ape is found in parts of North Africa as well as in the British colony of Gibraltar, 10 miles off Morocco's coast. *Barbary* is a term that once referred to North Africa from the Egyptian border to the Atlantic, including present-day Morocco.

Pink oleander blossoms flourish in many regions of Morocco. Although the beautiful flower is pleasant to the eye, oleander leaves are poisonous, and grazing goats and sheep avoid them.

Courtesy of Chris Loggers

13

Natural Resources

Phosphate rock, a key ingredient in fertilizers, is Morocco's greatest natural asset. The phosphate rock in Morocco and in the disputed Western Sahara is estimated to total two-thirds of the world's reserves. Morocco is the third largest producer of raw phosphates—after the United States and the Soviet Union—and it exports more than any other country. Morocco also has large deposits of lead, zinc, silver, and cobalt. The government has begun to stress development of these non-phosphate minerals to broaden the economic base of the country.

Geologists have uncovered significant deposits of oil shale—a type of slate from which oil can be extracted—outside Tangier and Tarfaya, a city near the Western Saharan border. Experts estimate that about 100 billion tons of oil shale exist in Morocco, and they hope to eventually extract over 200 billion barrels of oil. Morocco was also one of the first African nations to discover crude oil within its boundaries. By 1985, however, current wells had been depleted. As a result, many European and U.S. oil firms explore for oil off the shores of Morocco.

Natural gas was discovered in 1981 in the Essaouira Basin. Officials estimate that the find from this one site may eventually reduce national energy imports by 20 percent.

Courtesy of United Nations

Casablanca is Morocco's most important seaport. Its facilities and shipping capacity have expanded greatly since the country's independence in 1956.

Storks have made a nest in the minaret (tower) at Chellah in Rabat. The structure dates from the fourteenth century, when the Merinid dynasty (family of rulers) controlled the region.

Photo by Bernice K. Condit

Major Cities

Like many other Third World countries, Morocco has experienced huge migrations of rural dwellers to its newly Westernized cities. European-style high rises and increasing numbers of automobiles have pushed back the *derbs*, or ancient quarters. The appearance of bidonvilles (slums made up of makeshift shacks) is evidence of a severe shortage of affordable housing. A drought that began to affect rural areas in 1979 intensified the urban housing problem in the late 1980s and early 1990s. The Moroccan government has already invested $9 million in urban renewal efforts, including the construction of a huge housing project in Salé, near Rabat.

Rabat, with slightly over half a million inhabitants, is the capital of Morocco. The city was established in the thirteenth century, but it did not figure prominently in Moroccan affairs until the French occupation of the twentieth century. Rabat is now one of the largest manufacturing centers

Independent Picture Service

Seen from the height of an old wall, Rabat—the coastal city that became the capital of Morocco in 1913—displays its mixed Arab and European influences.

15

A row of new apartment buildings provides much-needed housing in Casablanca, whose population had swelled to 2.5 million in the early 1990s.

in the country and is known for its fine textiles and carpets.

Like many other national capitals, however, Rabat's chief business is government. The king's residence, one of the monarchy's grandest palaces, is located in the city. Rabat's official buildings display an architectural style that blends Moroccan and Spanish designs. Many of Rabat's wide streets are lined with palm trees and flowering shrubbery.

Casablanca is the industrial, commercial, and financial hub of Morocco. Its name means "white house" in Spanish. The

Some of Casablanca's low-income residents live in shanties (makeshift temporary dwellings).

Sections of the 500-year-old town of Chechaouèn, located in northern Morocco, have changed little since Muslims (followers of the Islamic religion) established the settlement as a secret base from which to attack Portuguese soldiers.

city is famous for its whitewashed buildings. Portuguese explorers founded the modern city in the sixteenth century on the ruins of an ancient settlement called Anfa. Warfare and earthquakes have destroyed the city several times, and European powers have rebuilt it twice. Modern Casablanca is the result of plans that were carried out under French and Spanish colonial administrations in the nineteenth century.

The largest urban center in Morocco, Casablanca is a city of extremes. New hotels and impressive commercial buildings stand in sharp contrast to the surrounding slums, where the urban poor live in temporary shelters. Although Casablanca is a rapidly growing industrial center—its population is estimated to be nearly 2.5 million —it cannot employ the thousands of workers who live in the slum areas because many of them lack specific technical skills.

Secondary Cities

In contrast to Rabat, which represents Morocco's government and administration, Fès (population 450,000) is the spiritual, intellectual, and artistic capital of the nation. Fès University is one of the best-known institutions in the Islamic world, and it draws students from the rest of North Africa as well as from Morocco itself. Beginning in the ninth century A.D., Muslim leaders beautified Fès with mosques (Islamic houses of worship) and other examples of Arab architecture.

Until Morocco achieved independence in 1956, Tangier was an international city occupied and governed by European administrators. Situated where Africa nearly touches Spain, Tangier faces the Strait of Gibraltar at the entrance to the Mediterranean Sea. Because of its strategic location, Tangier has long been of political importance and has attracted the interest of a number of European powers who sought to govern it. Modern Tangier, with over 280,000 inhabitants, is also a popular tourist resort.

Tangier is probably Morocco's oldest continuously inhabited city. Originally developed by the Phoenicians in the ninth century B.C., the northern port city was also home to Romans, Arabs, and Portuguese. In 1923 several European powers set aside Tangier as an international territory to prevent any single European nation from colonizing it. The various powers withdrew their authority over Tangier when it became part of independent Morocco in 1957.

At festivals throughout Morocco, men participate in fantasias, during which they ride in a mock battle charge, recalling their ancestors' military skill on horseback. Carrying ancient muskets, the riders charge two to three hundred yards at an accelerating gallop. At the end of the charge, the horsemen fire their muskets and rein in their horses, after which the crowd of onlookers cheers in appreciation.

2) History and Government

Archaeologists believe that 8,000 years ago the southern Sahara Desert was a fertile savanna (grassland) that supported large numbers of game and many hunters. Drastic changes in the area's climate slowly turned the savanna into desert.

After 4000 B.C., a late Stone-Age people continued to live and hunt along the northwestern coast of Africa. Around 2000 B.C., their descendants made contact with a people who had migrated westward to the Atlantic coastal plains. This new group, called the Berbers, established control over the vast Maghrib, including the area that is now Morocco.

The Berbers probably migrated from southwestern Asia into North Africa, near present-day Egypt. Language experts have tied the Berber dialects both to ancient Egyptian and to Asian languages. The trend of their findings supports the theory that the Berbers slowly crossed from the eastern to the western coast of Africa.

Phoenicians and Romans

The Phoenicians were seafaring merchants from present-day Lebanon. They founded a colony at Carthage, on the coast of what is now Tunisia, around the ninth century B.C. Phoenician rulers used this city as the cornerstone of their great empire, which included most of the lands of the Maghrib.

19

Located in northern Morocco, this ruin at Volubilis—a Roman city that dates from the second century A.D.—is all that remains of the residence of the Berber king, Juba II.

Photo by Maryknoll Missioners

Because the Phoenicians did not advance their settlements beyond Tangier, they often paid Berber leaders to protect their caravans in the African interior. The overall influence of the Phoenicians was relatively small, and the Berbers dominated the cultural life of Morocco until Roman times.

The Romans extended their territories through conquest, and by the first century A.D. their holdings included northern Morocco. They seized most of the best land

from the Berbers, dividing it up among Roman settlers. Berbers were given the choice of working as slaves for Roman landowners or of retreating to the hills. Many Berbers chose the mountainous Atlas regions, from which they staged frequent attacks on Roman outposts.

The Romans modernized Morocco by improving the ports, irrigating the land, and building roads and fortresses. They also introduced the riding camel during this period of economic expansion. The Romans soon used camel-mounted armies made up of Berber slaves. When Berber soldiers fought well, Roman emperors occasionally made them kings of Maghrib territory.

The Vandals and the Byzantines

By the fifth century A.D. Roman power was declining. Overtaxation, combined with poor management, helped to weaken the empire. A rebellious Roman official aided the Vandals—a northern European people who traveled to Morocco via Spain—in attacking North Africa in A.D. 429. Under their leader, Genseric, the Vandals overran the Maghrib and ruled Morocco for the next century. Berber raids on the new rulers continued as they had during the Roman period, but it was the military organization of the Byzantine Empire that was to drive the Vandals from Morocco.

Independent Picture Service

For centuries the camel has been one of the most important riding and draft (load-pulling) animals in Morocco and in other desert regions of northern Africa. The single-humped, or dromedary, camel is also found in western Asia. Its two-humped cousin can be seen in parts of western China and Mongolia.

Photo by Maryknoll Missioners

The Roman basilica at Volubilis served as both a court of justice and a place of public assembly.

Courtesy of Office National Marocain du Tourisme

Each year Muslims from all regions of Morocco travel to Moulay Idris—the Moroccan city named after the eighth-century Muslim leader. Located about 25 miles west of Fès, Moulay Idris welcome's thousands of pilgrims to honor the ruler.

The Byzantine state, or Eastern Roman Empire, had its capital at Constantinople in present-day Turkey. From there the emperor Justinian took control of the territories in North Africa. His army advanced into Morocco from the east, thus gaining a foothold in the eastern part of the country and along the Mediterranean coast.

Although he defeated the Vandals, Justinian had little support from the Berbers, or even from his own army, which he paid badly and treated harshly. Berber raiders, taking advantage of Justinian's weak administration, regained the land and held it until Arab armies attacked a century later.

Arab Invasion

As part of a highly organized religious crusade, Muslim armies—members of the Islamic faith founded by Muhammad in the early seventh century—came through the Taza Gap into present-day Morocco in A.D. 683. Control of the area was not secured until 710, when a Muslim Arab force under Musa ibn Nusayr conquered the Berbers who lived on the coastal plains. Berber groups living in the Atlas Mountains converted to Islam but remained free of Arab political control. In the four centuries that followed, Moroccans learned to speak a new language, absorbed the Arabs' Islamic religion, and came under a new government. Few traces remained of civilizations that had conquered them previously.

Musa ibn Nusayr raised a new army from his Berber converts and crossed the Strait of Gibraltar to invade Spain. The successful Arab and Berber soldiers settled in the new land, thus beginning the traditional mixing of Spanish and Moroccan styles sometimes referred to as Moorish culture.

Musa ibn Nusayr's conquest marked the high point of the Muslim religious expansion. In Morocco, however, Berbers of the Atlas Mountains continued to assert their independence, fighting both the Arabs and the Berbers of the plains, who had adopted Arab ways. It was not until the eighth century that an Arab, Moulay Idris Abdallah, was able to unite a group of western Berber peoples—known as the Awraba—thus bringing stability to Morocco.

A sharif, or direct descendant of Muhammad, Idris established the Awraba as the cornerstone of the first truly Moroccan state. Idris was assassinated in 792, but his son—Moulay Idris II—was able to hold the confederation together. He also founded the city of Fès in 808, and his descendants established borders that are still used to define Morocco's boundaries.

The Idrisids firmly established hereditary rule by sharifs descended from Muhammad. This religious law bound the

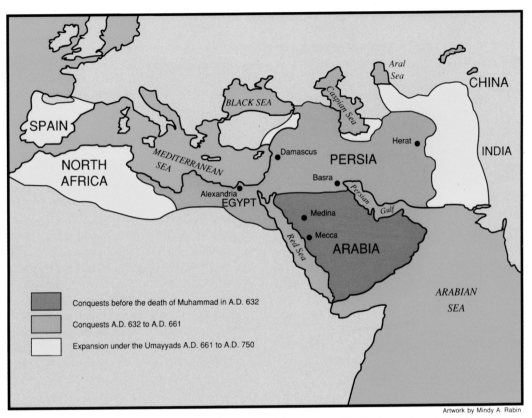

Artwork by Mindy A. Rabin

North Africa (including Morocco) was among the last regions to be conquered by Muslim armies, whose holdings eventually stretched from Western Europe to India.

Independent Picture Service

A traditional Moorish archway graces the entrance to this Andalusian mosque at Fès. *Andalusian* refers to the region of Andalusia, located in southern Spain.

dynasty together until Moulay Idris II divided his state into equal parts to be ruled by his sons. These smaller kingdoms attacked one another and, in turn, were attacked by the Berbers of the Atlas Mountains and by Muslim armies from Spain. In the tenth century, an Islamic emir (prince) from Cordoba, Spain, captured northern Morocco.

Newcomers from the East and the Beginning of Berber Unity

In the mid-eleventh century, a nomadic Arab people from northeastern Africa migrated to Morocco and to other regions of the Maghrib. For 200 years, this group converted much of the Berber-held farmland into pasture for their herds. Some Berbers adopted the wandering lifestyle of the newcomers, and others joined the Berbers of the Atlas Mountains.

23

Considered one of the greatest examples of Almohad artistic achievement, the minaret of the Koutoubia Mosque in Marrakech rises to over 250 feet, and its exterior decorations are different on each face. Koutoubia derives from an Arabic phrase meaning "mosque of the bookshops." Bookstalls once lined both sides of the street leading to the mosque.

During the initial period of this migration to Morocco, however, Berbers experienced a revival of their power and religious authority, which united them for the first time as a political force. Three loose unions—the Sanhaja, the Masmouda, and the Zenata—had formed by the beginning of the eleventh century. Taking religious soldiers from Berber families, three successive dynasties—the Almoravid, the Almohad, and the Merinid—held power until the fourteenth century. Each funded its government through control of the area's profitable trade in salt and gold.

Early in the eleventh century, Sanhaja leaders accepted a strict Muslim teacher named ibn Yasin as their spiritual head. Yasin established a well-protected holy place called a ribat and named his Sanhaja students the Almoravids, or men of the ribat.

Although the Almoravids wanted to spread a stricter form of Islam, the Sanhaja armies also wished to overcome the Zenata group, who competed with the Sanhaja for trade. By the end of the eleventh century, the Almoravids controlled the northwestern quarter of the African continent and part of Spain. (Morocco's current claim to the Western Sahara is based on the boundaries established during Almoravid rule.) The Almoravids took Marrakech as their capital but allowed local leaders to retain power.

By the twelfth century, however, Almoravid leaders came to accept a looser interpretation of the Koran (Islamic holy writings), and the Sanhaja troops, who still favored a stricter code, rebelled. Another religious reform group—the Almohads—overpowered the Almoravid dynasty during its struggle with the Sanhaja.

Like the Almoravids, the Almohads controlled a portion of Spain and began to loosen their strict interpretation of Koranic laws. Eventually the dynasty moved its base of power from North Africa to Spain. The intellectual and artistic advances of Almohads in Spain helped to

At the Atlantic coastal city of Al-Jadida, centuries-old Portuguese cannons are still poised as if ready for battle. The Portuguese founded the present-day seaside resort in 1502, naming it Mazagan.

foster a rebirth of the arts in Christian Europe during the fourteenth and fifteenth centuries. By the thirteenth century, however, the Almohads had lost power to a third dynasty—the Merinids—which was composed of Arab-influenced Berbers who had rebelled against the Almohads in 1212.

The leaders of the anti-Almohad rebellion formed the Merinid dynasty, which became dominant in Morocco by capturing Marrakech in 1271. The Merinids created a new capital, Rabat, on the site of a captured Almohad fortress.

Trade and art flourished under the Merinids, and gold and salt were the dynasty's chief sources of revenue. The Merinids were unable, however, to extend the borders of their state as far as the previous Berber dynasties.

A renewal of Christian European power ended Merinid rule when the Portuguese seized Ceuta in 1415 and used the port to launch an attack on the entire region. At the same time, Christian armies of northern Spain regained southern Spain from the Muslims.

European Offensives

Christian armies from Spain and Portugal had invaded Morocco by the beginning of the sixteenth century, but they made only limited attempts to strengthen their rule. The natural resources of the newly discovered Americas were of more immediate interest to the Spanish and the Portuguese.

Nevertheless, Spain and Portugal occupied strategic ports on the northern coasts of Morocco and established control of the sea routes within the western Mediterranean. Portuguese troops raided Berber camps, and Portuguese ships attacked small Arab vessels off the coast. During the sixteenth century, and for several centuries thereafter, European forces captured and lost these ports many times. No European force, however, permanently controlled the interior of Morocco.

The Saadians and the Alawis

Although peoples in some parts of the Maghrib accepted a strict form of Islam, many others followed the teachings of marabouts, or wandering holy men. Marabouts were especially popular among isolated Berber groups. In the sixteenth century the marabouts selected an Arab group with blood ties to Muhammad—the Saadians—to lead a jihad, or holy war, against the Christians in Morocco.

The first effective Saadi leader was Ahmed al-Mansur, whose soldiers reclaimed Ceuta, among other strategic points. Al-Mansur adopted administrative methods from the Ottoman Turks of southwestern Asia to govern his newly captured territory. Pashas, or governors, were left to rule each area and were supported by a caid, or tax collector, who had enough military strength to police the area. The leader of this ruling dynasty came to be called a sultan.

Courtesy of Cultural and Tourism Office of the Turkish Embassy

Adopting the Turkish model of administration, the Moroccan sultan also enjoyed absolute power within his realm. Here, a sultan meets with a group of his advisers.

In 1591 al-Mansur sent an expedition across the Sahara Desert into the present-day nations of Mali and Algeria to capture people for his slave trade, as well as to search for gold mines. Although members of the expedition failed to locate mines, they did establish forts at desert positions, such as Tombouctou. These outposts en-

Courtesy of National Maritime Museum

As Spanish and Portuguese ships began to land on Moroccan shores in the 1500s, Muslim and Christian naval forces engaged in frequent battles in the Mediterranean. In addition, Muslim corsairs, or pirates, sailed the Mediterranean and North Atlantic seas, raiding European coastal towns and attacking Christian pirate ships. The port of Salé along Morocco's northwestern coast served as an important base for corsairs, whose presence continued into the early part of the nineteenth century.

This ornately designed verse from a Koran (Islamic book of sacred writings) dates from the sixteenth century and is written in classical Arabic script. Moroccan sultans studied the Koran for political as well as for personal guidance.

abled al-Mansur to transport slaves across the desert. During al-Mansur's reign, Morocco also became one of the continent's leading centers of trade in spices, cloth, and ivory.

After the death of al-Mansur, weak successors could not prevent pashas and marabouts from rebelling, and disorder increased. In the 100 years of Saadi rule, 8 of the 12 sultans who ruled were assassinated. The Alawis, who had migrated from Arabia during the reign of the fourteenth-century Merinid dynasty, came to power at this time and fought the mara-

bouts in another jihad. Like the earlier followers of Idris, the Alawis believed in rule by sharifs, who were descended from Muhammad.

Moulay Ismail and His Successors

In 1672 Moulay Ismail succeeded his brother, Moulay Rashid, and reigned as the Alawite sultan for 55 years. His descendants still rule present-day Morocco.

Ismail organized the Alawite kingdom so successfully that the Ottoman Turks—who had extended their influence from

Courtesy of Chris Loggers

The mountains of Morocco have figured in its history for centuries, either as protection against invading armies or as the scene of the development of new ruling powers.

modern-day Turkey across southwestern Asia and most of North Africa—were unable to gain control of Morocco. The western boundary of the Ottoman Empire, therefore, stopped at Morocco's borders. The Alawite sultan, however, saw the value in European contacts and exchanged diplomats with France—a decision that marked the beginning of French influence in Morocco.

Rulers who succeeded Ismail lost the control that he had exerted over the Berber groups in the High Atlas Mountains and commanded only small, ineffective military forces. Although the Alawis remained in power, their area of control grew smaller.

European Takeover

By the end of the nineteenth century, a rush by European countries to claim African lands—sometimes called the "scramble for Africa"—had begun. Each major power claimed vast sections of the African continent and sought to secure its claims through treaties with local leaders. The Europeans sought to use Moroccan ports to ensure passage through the Strait of Gibraltar to markets in the Western Hemisphere. Despite European interest and competition, however, Morocco was one of the last African states to come under foreign control.

Both Spain and France already had investments in Morocco. French manufacturers had operated in Morocco's larger cities since the beginning of the nineteenth century, and Spain had forts in the Ceuta area prior to the 1800s. France insisted on ruling in Morocco, but the other major powers demanded some of France's other African territory in exchange. Thus Germany received part of French Equatorial Africa, Britain confirmed its control in Egypt, and Italy agreed to take Libya. Spain, however, continued to claim a part of Morocco.

Sultan Abd al-Aziz had neither the military strength nor the regional unity needed to resist the Europeans. French forces occupied Morocco in 1907, and the entrance of the French army marked the end of Moroccan independence.

The sultan's brother, Moulay Abd al-Hafid, ousted al-Aziz and became the nation's leader in 1908. On March 30, 1912, Sultan al-Hafid signed the Treaty of Fès, which made Morocco a French protectorate. Later in the year, the Spanish signed a similar document, which gave them control over the previously French-dominated northern coast and Rif Massif. To ensure that the Strait of Gibraltar would remain open, the strategic port of Tangier was established as an international zone to be administered by the other interested European powers.

Fès served as Morocco's capital during three separate periods over the last 12 centuries.

TANGIER

MOROCCO ALGERIA TUNISIA

IFNI

RIO DE ORO

LIBYA EGYPT

FRENCH

WEST AFRICA

GAMBIA ANGLO-
EGYPTIAN
SUDAN ERITREA

PORT.
GUINEA

FRENCH
EQUATORIAL
AFRICA FR. TER.
AFARS/ISSAS

SIERRA
LEONE GOLD
COAST NIGERIA ABYSSINIA

LIBERIA

TOGOLAND CAMEROONS BRITISH
SOMALILAND

SPANISH GUINEA UGANDA ITALIAN
SOMALILAND

GABON BELGIAN
CONGO KENYA

GERMAN
EAST
AFRICA ZANZIBAR

NYASALAND

ANGOLA COMORO
IS.

NO.
RHODESIA

SOUTH-
WEST
AFRICA SO.
RHODESIA

WALVIS BAY BECHUANA-
LAND

PORT. EAST AFRICA

MADAGASCAR

UNION
OF SOUTH
AFRICA

BASUTOLAND

FRANCE	ITALY
GREAT BRITAIN	SPAIN
PORTUGAL	BELGIUM
GERMANY	INDEPENDENT STATES

Artwork by Larry Kaushansky

By the late nineteenth century, European powers had carved the continent of Africa into areas of influence. France, Spain, and Germany each had an interest in Moroccan territory, but present-day Morocco became a French protectorate in 1912. Map information taken from *The Anchor Atlas of World History,* 1978.

Early Colonial Rule

The first French resident-general in Morocco was Louis-Hubert-Gonzalve Lyautey. Lyautey trained his staff to function within Morocco's existing Islamic institutions. He believed that the French should strengthen the sultan's central government and its control over the various Berber groups in the mountain regions. This policy, he felt, would eventually allow the French to leave Morocco in the hands of a local government that was both secure and pro-French.

Under Lyautey, France built schools, hospitals, bridges, and other much-needed improvements for Morocco. The colonial government trained Moroccans for official posts in the French-run administration. Within two years the resident-general had unified the region of central Morocco, from Fès to Marrakech.

In 1921 the Spanish colonial forces in northern Morocco tried to subdue the Berbers of the Rif Massif with a force of 20,000 men. The isolated Berbers joined together under Abd al-Krim, a scholar and a skilled military leader. Al-Krim resisted the Spanish forces and established the Rif Republic, an independent state governed by Moroccan Berbers and Arabs. In 1924 al-Krim's forces threatened to move into French Morocco. Lyautey managed to put down the rebellion and to capture part of Spanish Morocco, but the Rif Republic became a symbol of the Moroccan people's desire for independence.

The Rise of Nationalism

Against Lyautey's wishes, thousands of French settlers (called colons) moved into Morocco during the early 1900s. Through pressure from the colons, official French policy in Morocco changed from one of aiding the Moroccan government to one of weakening it. After Lyautey left his post in 1925, the French educational system—which did not teach Arabic or Islam—was introduced for Moroccan children. Protectorate officials began to support selected pashas and marabouts, hoping to weaken the sultan's authority.

Two independent nationalist groups formed to resist French authority. The first was made up of Moroccan students from the colleges and schools that Lyautey had founded. Initially, this academic group of nationalists sought only to reform the French system, but later they formed the Istiqlal (Freedom) party and pressed for independence.

Independent Picture Service

Like his predecessors, Mohammed V was a direct descendant of the prophet Muhammad.

Students enrolled at a traditional Arab university in Fès ran the second nationalist group. Called the Salafiya, this group had been trained in ancient Arab traditions and in a strict form of Islam. They wanted to weaken the influence of the pro-French marabouts and to establish Morocco's independence.

The nationalist cause was greatly helped by Mohammed V, whom the French had appointed as sultan in 1927. The French intended Mohammed V, who was only 17

31

years old, to be a defender of their colonial policies. In public speeches, however, Mohammed V referred to the rights of the Moroccan people and to their long history of independence prior to French intervention.

In addition to speaking on nationalist topics, the sultan signed the Plan of Reforms submitted to him in 1934 by nationalist leaders. This move angered the French but gained Mohammed V support throughout the nation. Anti-French demonstrations and riots occurred frequently in Morocco in the 1930s.

Independence

The end of World War II in 1945 brought new strength to the nationalist movement in Africa. Because Morocco had resisted the Axis (pro-German) forces throughout the war and had served as a base for Britain and the United States, Mohammed V hoped that the Allies (anti-German nations) would also support Moroccan independence. This hope was strengthened when Morocco's leader met with Britain's prime minister Winston Churchill and with U.S. president Franklin Roosevelt at the Casablanca Conference in 1943.

The French resident-general tried to stop the sultan's efforts by forcing him to sign *zahirs,* or royal orders, that would limit the sultan's power. (The terms of the 1912 Treaty of Fès had made zahirs necessary to alter the Moroccan government.) For six years Mohammed V refused to sign any zahirs that would weaken either the nationalist movement or his own position.

The French eventually replaced the sultan with an elderly relative—Mulay Ben Arafa—whom they could better control. In

Courtesy of Franklin D. Roosevelt Library

U.S. president Franklin Roosevelt *(left)* and British prime minister Winston Churchill consult at the Casablanca Conference in 1943. The location of the conference gave Mohammed V the opportunity to meet with the two Western leaders, who he hoped would agree to support Moroccan independence.

Morocco has used a red flag for centuries, choosing different emblems as the central focus. After independence in 1956, the flag that had been introduced in 1915—featuring the green pentacle, or five-pointed star—was officially adopted. Green is the traditional color of Islam, and red represents the freedom of the Moroccan people.

1953 Mohammed V and his family were exiled to the island of Madagascar off the coast of southeastern Africa. Moroccan reaction was strong, and violence and rioting broke out in the nation. Even rural groups, which had previously shown little interest in politics, became involved.

Spurred by this national reaction, the membership of the Istiqlal party grew to 80,000 in the early 1950s. Even Berber groups, some of which had previously supported the French, joined the more radical members of Istiqlal. The Army of National Liberation grew out of this membership and turned to violent action. During the two years of the sultan's exile, members of the army killed several hundred French settlers.

To quiet the situation, the French returned Mohammed V to Morocco in 1955.

Mohammed V's profile is depicted on a silver dirham coin. On its reverse side, two dates of issue are found—the Gregorian (which uses the months January through December) and the Islamic (whose months are based on the lunar cycle). The Islamic year 1 began with the prophet Muhammad's escape from Mecca and is the equivalent of the Gregorian year A.D. 622.

An aerial view of Salé, which is just across the Bou Regreg River from Rabat, includes a portion of a mosque and its towering minaret. The initial construction of this mosque dates from the twelfth-century Almohad dynasty.

On November 6 of that year, France agreed to end the protectorate and to recognize Morocco as an independent nation. On March 2, 1956, Mohammed V and his new government began their administration of independent Morocco.

Early Moroccan Policy

Mohammed V wanted to continue Morocco's relationship with France after independence. He felt that the country needed French technical and economic assistance to survive its early years. But the members of his government, especially those from the Istiqlal party, wanted complete separation from France. Istiqlal ministers pushed for the creation of a one-party state, hoping to assume control of the new regime.

Mohammed V, however, enjoyed great popular support. Moroccans saw him both as a royal figure and as a hero of the independence movement. Because of this popularity, the sultan ruled without a written constitution for his six years as head of independent Morocco. From 1956 to 1961 he increased the power of the monarchy by making sure that no single party ever controlled the government.

In 1957 Mohammed V gave himself the European title of king and appointed his son, Mulay Hassan, crown prince, or successor to the throne. In 1958 Morocco joined the Arab League—a group of Arab states dedicated to Arab unity—but Mohammed V made a determined effort to preserve Morocco's neutral international position. For example, Morocco accepted financial and military aid from both the United States and the Soviet Union.

The king badly damaged relations with Morocco's neighbors, however, with his claims to a "Greater Morocco." Mohammed V, along with many of his subjects, felt that Morocco was entitled to the former Spanish colony of the Western Sahara —and to territories in present-day Mauritania and Mali—because of boundaries established in the tenth and eleventh centuries. In the case of the Algerian-Moroccan border, both countries claimed the territory between Béchar and Tindouf because the French colonial administration had never clearly divided the region.

Soon this issue threatened to separate Morocco from both the African and Arab worlds. Consequently, Mohammed V gave up his claims to all of the disputed regions except the Western Sahara. Partly because of this new stance, Morocco was invited in January 1963 to join the newly formed Organization of African Unity (OAU), a group of moderate African states.

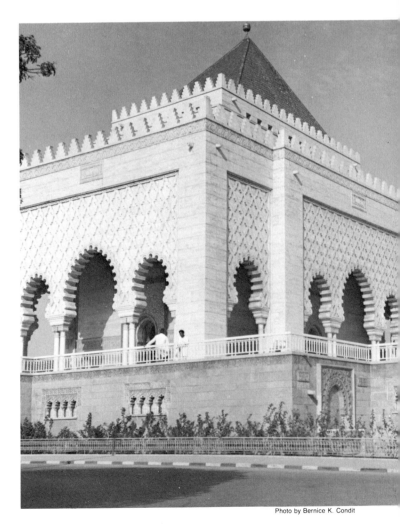

King Hassan II had this mausoleum (above-ground tomb) built in Rabat for his father, Mohammed V.

Photo by Bernice K. Condit

35

Hassan II continues to encourage expansion of industry while also restoring many historic structures. In this way he maintains a sense of the nation's long heritage within a changing environment.

Courtesy of Embassy of Morocco

King Hassan II

One month after the first OAU conference, Mohammed V died from complications following surgery. His son, Crown Prince Mulay Hassan, left his post as chief of staff of the Moroccan Air Force and assumed the throne as King Hassan II. The new king reassured Moroccans that he would carry out the policies of his father.

In December 1962 Hassan II drafted a constitution that was overwhelmingly approved by the Moroccan people. The document safeguarded his royal powers and created a two-house legislature. But the new constitution failed to produce a stable government. Istiqlal party members continued to demand limitations on the king's powers. The legislature voted down laws and reforms that the king drafted, and these actions in turn met with great resistance from Hassan II.

In 1965 student protests in Casablanca resulted in frequent riots. Demonstrators demanded changes in a new law requiring all students over 17 years of age to take technical training. Police and army forces killed more than 400 people. Hassan II blamed the Casablanca riots on the ineffective legislative system and declared a state of emergency. During this period, the king assumed the prime minister's duties and appointed a new cabinet.

In 1967 the king supplied three army battalions to Egypt during the Six-Day War between the Arab world and Israel—a Jewish state on the eastern shores of the Mediterranean that is surrounded by Arab neighbors. Although the Moroccan troops arrived too late to fight, Hassan's efforts cemented ties with the Arab nations of the Middle East. At home, however, the king protected Moroccan Jews who became targets for Arab terrorists during the war. In addition, Hassan's government officially condemned a countrywide boycott against Moroccan Jewish businesses. The boycott was driving thousands of Jews to Israel and France.

In 1970 the king passed another constitution by popular vote. Over 98 percent of Moroccan voters supported the new document, which increased the powers of

Courtesy of Israel Government Press Office

Israeli forces captured Egyptian territory during the Six-Day War in 1967. A plan adopted at a meeting of Arab states at Fès in 1982 suggested that these states would recognize Israel if Israel withdrew from the lands it had acquired during the war.

their king. After the selection of the new one-house legislature, Hassan II ended the state of emergency, which had been in effect for five years.

The Modern Era

Between 1971 and 1972 two attempted coups—both engineered by important government and military officials—revealed growing dissatisfaction within the royal administration. In response, Hassan II instituted a reorganization plan aimed at tightening national security. The king assumed control of the armed forces and, after a series of terrorist attacks in 1973, outlawed several radical political parties.

Hassan II turned his attention again to the Western Sahara, which he still hoped

Photo by Daniel H. Condit

A modern, landscaped city center reflects Casablanca's recent history of Western influence. Industrialization has brought prosperity to the more developed sections of this port city.

to claim for Morocco. After Spain withdrew its forces from the disputed territory in 1975, Hassan II organized the Green March—an event that brought together 350,000 Moroccans who marched into the Western Sahara carrying green Islamic banners and Korans. Eventually, Moroc-co committed over 75 percent of its weaponry and troops to fighting the Polisario—an Algerian-backed force fighting for self-rule in the Western Sahara.

Morocco's economy faced hard times. A drought ruined harvests across the countryside, and by 1980 production of grains

Holding his Koran and a Moroccan flag, a member of the November 1975 Green March enters what was then the Spanish-held Western Sahara. After the marchers withdrew on November 9, Spain ceased its administrative role, and Morocco and Mauritania shared authority. In 1979, however, Mauritania signed a peace treaty with the Polisario—an Algerian-backed guerrilla movement—and left the territory.

The white-walled royal palace—situated at the southern edge of Rabat—is surrounded by a complex of buildings, some of which house members of King Hassan's family. Other structures serve as quarters for visiting dignitaries or as barracks for soldiers in the king's Royal Guard and their families.

had fallen by 65 percent. In addition, the world market for phosphates—one of Morocco's chief exports—dropped drastically. Finally, the war in the Western Sahara drained much of Morocco's revenues away from social and industrial projects.

Because of its policy regarding the Western Sahara, Morocco cooled its relations with its neighbors, including Algeria and Libya, in the 1980s. Libya no longer supports the efforts of the Polisario, but Algeria still backs the movement for self-rule in the disputed territory. Morocco and Algeria resumed diplomatic relations in 1989 in the hope of fostering a resolution to the war.

In the 1990s, prospects seem strong for a peaceful settlement of the conflict. A United Nations' plan for a public vote to decide the future of the Western Sahara is moving forward. The question to be posed in the vote is whether the territory wants to become part of Morocco or to become independent. Morocco has agreed to abide by the decision of the Western Saharans, and the United Nations will monitor the vote.

Government

Morocco's Constitution of 1972, drafted by Hassan II, limits the power of the throne, placing much of the nation's administration in the hands of an elected government. A special clause, however, allows the king to take complete control in cases of national emergency. The document also makes the king's son his legal successor.

Because political parties are allowed, the government is not an absolute monarchy. On the other hand, the country is not a democracy since the king still retains extensive powers. As head of state, the king of Morocco appoints a prime minister, with whom he shares the power to author legislation. A council of ministers, whose members are also selected individually by the king, includes representatives of several parties as well as persons without political ties. Morocco's bicameral (two-house) legislature has a limited role in budgetary reviews and in approval of laws sponsored by the king or the prime minister.

Morocco's judicial system is technically independent, but it is heavily influenced by the king, who appoints judges to the national supreme court and also presides over a supreme council of the judiciary. This council supervises Morocco's courts. The national legal system is based on separate Islamic and Judaic codes and on traditional Berber law. Local leaders operate Islamic courts in their communities.

A bird's-eye view shows a bustling street scene in Morocco's capital city, Rabat.

3) The People

Arabs and Berbers make up 98 percent of Morocco's 25.6 million people. Harratines and Moroccan Jews comprise the remaining 2 percent. A group originally located in the area south of the Western Sahara, the Harratines have historically worked as agricultural laborers for Berber farmers. Moroccan Jews at one time numbered more

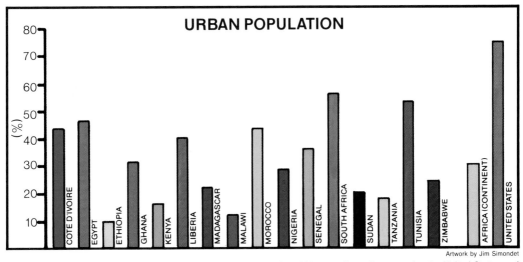

URBAN POPULATION

(%)

COTE D'IVOIRE · EGYPT · ETHIOPIA · GHANA · KENYA · LIBERIA · MADAGASCAR · MALAWI · MOROCCO · NIGERIA · SENEGAL · SOUTH AFRICA · SUDAN · TANZANIA · TUNISIA · ZIMBABWE · AFRICA (CONTINENT) · UNITED STATES

Artwork by Jim Simondet

Illustrated here are the percentages of the urban populations of 16 African nations. Averages for the United States and the entire continent of Africa are included for comparison. Data taken from "1987 World Population Data Sheet."

than 200,000, but political events in the 1950s caused many to leave. In the early 1990s, less than 14,000 Jews resided in the country. After independence, the number of Europeans in Morocco also dwindled considerably.

Close to 50 percent of Morocco's population resides in urban centers. The number of average-sized cities—those having populations of 20,000 to 100,000—tripled between 1965 and 1985.

Morocco's population has been growing at an annual rate of 2.6 percent. Although this figure is low for Africa in general, it indicates that at the present rate the nation's population will double in 27 years. Like many African nations, Morocco's population is very young—42 percent are under 15 years of age, while only 4 percent are over 65.

Berbers and Arabs

Although Arabic is the official Moroccan language and although Islam is the official religion, Berber dialects and traditions survive. The term "Berber" has long been applied to groups who have dominated the

Photo by Robert W. Nelson

This Moroccan from Marrakech shares his heritage with the Berbers of the Atlas Mountains, which rise just beyond the city.

41

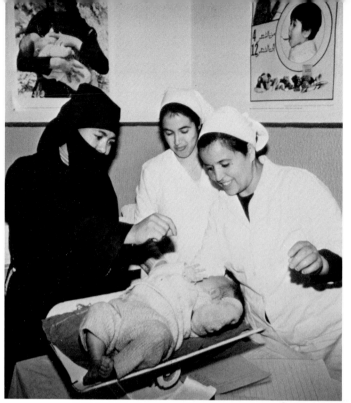

A mother holds her child's attention as the infant is weighed at a Moroccan health clinic.

mountainous regions of the Maghrib. From the seventh century onward, however, Arab populations mixed extensively with Berber societies.

As a result, it is difficult to separate Arabs from Berbers who have adopted Arab culture. The distinctions made by scholars are often geographic. The Atlas Mountains of Morocco are still home to people who converse in a distinct Berber language, while the coastal plains are dominated by Arabic-speakers.

In modern times, Arab political influence has increased in both the political and economic sectors. The Moroccan government has tried to unify the country by imposing Arab institutions on the entire population. This move, however, has led to resentment. Berber spokespeople point out that the policy favors Arabs in the strong urban competition for employment or advancement.

Berber culture is founded on regional groups that are often formed by family ties rather than by any general ethnic identity. The many distinct Berber societies can be divided geographically into three major groupings. The Rifians occupy the north, the Berraber live in the center of the country and in the Sahara, and the Shluh inhabit the Middle Atlas and the High Atlas mountains.

Health

Morocco's medical services are partially a result of European rule. French officials introduced a basic health-care program in 1912, but it mainly served Europeans. A public health department was set up in 1926 to address the needs of Moroccans more directly. Morocco's current Ministry of Public Health, expanding on the foundation laid down by the French, has made great progress in solving the nation's severe health problems.

Poor sanitation and unclean water—combined with problems caused by urban overcrowding—are at the root of the nation's high infant mortality rate and low life expectancy. Roughly 82 infants die out of every 1,000 live births, and life ex-

Efforts continue to provide children in rural areas—such as these school-boys from Imouzzer in southwestern Morocco—with greater access to health facilities.

Photo by Bernice K. Condit

pectancy is 61 years. The most common causes of death among children are measles, tetanus, and whooping cough. Infant vaccination has become a government priority. Among adults, tuberculosis and gonorrhea (a sexually transmitted disease) are often fatal.

The Ministry of Public Health has been successful in fighting most epidemic diseases. Health officials wiped out bubonic plague in 1945 and smallpox some years later. Typhus, malaria, and tuberculosis are still present in Morocco, but mobile medical teams and rural clinics have sharply reduced fatal cases.

The government has set aside 7 percent of the national budget for training doctors and nurses, and more than half of Morocco's health professionals live and practice in urban areas. In the cities, approximately one hospital bed exists for every 610 people. In the nation's remote areas, by contrast, the ratio is one bed per 3,010 inhabitants.

Courtesy of UNICEF

High-school girls share the use of a microscope in their science class.

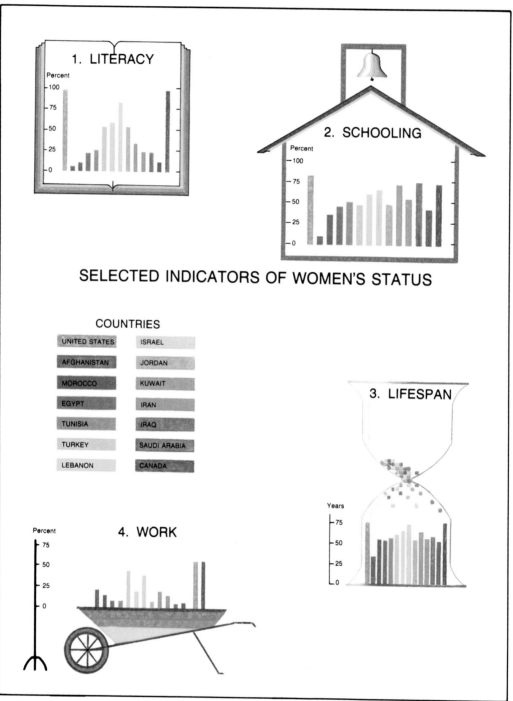

1. LITERACY

Percent

2. SCHOOLING

Percent

SELECTED INDICATORS OF WOMEN'S STATUS

COUNTRIES

UNITED STATES	ISRAEL
AFGHANISTAN	JORDAN
MOROCCO	KUWAIT
EGYPT	IRAN
TUNISIA	IRAQ
TURKEY	SAUDI ARABIA
LEBANON	CANADA

3. LIFESPAN

Years

4. WORK

Percent

Artwork by Carol F. Barrett

Depicted in this chart are factors relating to the status of women in the Middle East, southwestern Asia, and North Africa. Graph 1, labeled Literacy, shows the percentage of adult women who can read and write. Graph 2 illustrates the proportion of school-aged girls who actually attend elementary and secondary schools. Graph 3 depicts the life expectancy of female babies at birth. Graph 4 shows the percentage of women in the income-producing work force. Data taken from *Women in the World: An International Atlas,* 1986 and from *Women . . . A World Survey,* 1985.

The holy writings of Muslim countries are penned in Arabic, which is read from right to left. This ornate example—an Arabic script known as Taliq—was produced in Turkey during the nineteenth century.

Language and Literature

Moroccan Arabic is not identical to the Arabic spoken in other parts of the world. For example, a Moroccan could understand a Syrian, but with difficulty. Mostly a spoken language, Moroccan Arabic is rarely used for literary purposes. The classical Arabic of the Koran dominates Morocco's written tradition and is used almost exclusively in the press.

Because the government is promoting the use of Arabic in Morocco's schools, each year fewer Moroccans speak Berber dialects. Many Berbers who work in cities —as well as Berber schoolchildren—learn Arabic but speak the Berber language when they go back to their homes. Over 50 percent of Berber men speak either Arabic or French. Far fewer Berber women are bilingual, because they often remain in rural villages while their husbands migrate to the cities. Traditional Berber dialects include Rifi in the north, Tamazight in central Morocco, and Tashilhit in the High Atlas Mountains.

French is the most common language of modern Moroccan literature, although a

A stop sign in Arabic is recognizable to non-Arabic speakers by its universal shape and color.

few Arabic novels have been published. Morocco's Allal al-Fassi produced beautiful Arabic verse in the years following World War I. Abdulhamid Benjelloun is considered one of the finest novelists working in traditional Arabic. He is admired for his novel *Memories of Childhood* as well as for his collections of short stories, which draw upon his personal experiences as a high government official. Driss Charibi and Ahmed Sefrioui are two of Morocco's most notable authors in French. Both writers examine the conflicting influences of religion, progress, and foreign intervention in their country.

Education

Before 1912, schooling for most Moroccans consisted of two or three years of religious training. After 1912 the French set up French-style schools, which taught thousands of Moroccans each year. French classes, however, neglected Arab traditions and language. As a result of this omission, the Moroccan government has stressed Arab culture in the nation's schools since gaining independence.

By the mid-1970s, the Ministry of National Education had replaced almost all French instructors with Moroccans and had established Arabic as the academic language. Critics within the educational system have charged that the Ministry of National Education is ignoring the Berber language. Nevertheless, the ministry plans to have all schools teaching in Arabic by the 1990s.

In 1990 more than 70 percent of Moroccan children aged 7 to 13 were enrolled in primary schools. The five-year program stresses Arabic and religious training from the Koran. Children spend about 10 hours per week studying French, which is still regarded as a valuable second language.

Less than half of Morocco's primary school students go on to secondary school. One million children were enrolled in the six-year secondary program in the early

Photo by Bernice K. Condit

Students mingle between classes at one of Rabat's universities.

Courtesy of UNICEF

At a woodworking class, a young student puts the finishing touches on his creation.

Courtesy of UNICEF

As a learning tool, a primary-school teacher provides a drawing of what each Arabic word represents.

1990s. French becomes more important at the high school level, since mathematics and science are still taught in that language. Teachers use Arabic for history, geography, and additional religious instruction. In 1990 about 34 percent of Moroccan men and about 3 percent of Moroccan women were literate.

Morocco has six universities, and their combined enrollments totaled 118,000 in the early 1990s. More than half of these students attend universities in the Rabat area. Twenty-four schools provide advanced vocational training for about 8,000 students. An additional 30,000 Moroccans attend institutions abroad.

Courtesy of UNICEF

Girls play an outdoor game of basketball during gym class.

In Marrakech, detailed wood carvings decorate the sixteenth-century tombs of leaders of the Saadi dynasty.

The Ali ibn Yusuf Mosque honors the Almoravid leader who brought Marrakech to prominence early in the twelfth century. Among the constructions begun under Ali ibn Yusuf's rule was an underground system of channels designed to carry water to the city's palm trees.

By the beginning of the twentieth century, the Saadi tombs lay partly in ruins. They have since been restored, and their lavishly carved surfaces display geometric patterns—in the Islamic artistic tradition—and verses from the Koran.

The Arts

Moroccan, or Moorish, architecture originated in Muslim Spain in the eighth century. Arab and Berber religious conquerors returned to Morocco with Spanish designs, which were then adopted and developed by artisans throughout North Africa. Historically, most artistic efforts were devoted to the building of mosques and religious schools. Mosques often have horseshoe-shaped arches, windows, and doorways as well as slender columns and large outdoor courtyards. French styles are also a part of Morocco's architectural heritage. Urban business and residential sections, which were begun under French rule, use many European materials and designs.

Independent Picture Service

A leather craftsperson works with concentration on his skillfully decorated handiwork.

Courtesy of United Nations

An ensemble in Fès performs with European and traditional instruments. Here, some of the musicians play violins, which rest on their knees.

Moroccan craftspeople are world famous for their skills in making items of fine leather. After 1900, when European manufacturers duplicated the look of Moroccan leather and began to produce it at much cheaper prices, the demand for handmade leather goods decreased in other Western nations and in Morocco itself. The government has tried to revive the industry by inspecting leather goods to ensure their uniformly high quality. In addition, schools have trained artisans to make articles that are commercially valuable outside of Morocco.

Painting traditionally was a purely decorative art in Morocco, and some of the finest work is found on the tile walls of mosques. By the early 1960s, however, Moroccan painters, such as Favid Belkahia and Ahmed Yacoubi, departed from the strict Islamic tradition that forbids artwork using human images. Although most of the nation's painters still depict scenes from nature, more and more have turned to scenes of people and street life.

This man follows tradition by leaving his shoes at the entrance of a mosque. Muslims are expected to pray five times each day.

Photo by Jenny Matthews

Most classical Moroccan music dates from the tenth to the fourteenth centuries. Students spend many years at music conservatories in Rabat and Marrakech learning both theory and technique. An ensemble might include a *darbuqa* (a funnel-shaped drum), a *tar* (a kind of tambourine), a rebab (a lute-shaped instrument), and a kemancha (a violin that usually has only one string).

Popular Moroccan music features both Berber and Arab elements. *Griha* is the most widely played popular music, often combining the sounds of a viola and a two-stringed mandolin. Dancing—an important part of harvests, marriages, and funerals —usually features heavy rhythms provided by drums and tambourines.

Religion

About 99 percent of Morocco's people are Muslims. Both Arabs and Berbers practice Islam in their daily lives; Berber groups may also include elements of folk religion in their beliefs. Many of the urban poor have turned to the worship of famous figures of Islam, whom they regard as saints. Although this practice goes against strict Islamic tradition—under which all

Muslims are held to be equal—the Islamic leadership in Morocco has taken a neutral position on the cult of saints.

Most Moroccans are members of the Sunni sect of the Islamic religion. Several duties, sometimes called pillars of faith, are required of Sunni Muslims. The three most demanding duties are daily prayer, fasting, and pilgrimage. A Muslim must pray five times each day—at dawn, midday, midafternoon, sunset, and nightfall. Throughout the holy month of Ramadan, Muslims must not eat, drink, or smoke during daylight hours. Finally, Muslim men are required to visit the holy city of Mecca in Saudi Arabia at least once in their lifetime, if they are physically able.

Food

The average Moroccan lives on a diet of vegetables, goat and mutton meat, barley or wheat flour, and milk. Moroccan meals may vary from simple couscous—a steamed wheat dish that is served with meat and vegetables—to elaborate pigeon or chicken pies. Meat pies can take as long as eight hours to prepare because the fillings are enclosed in as many as 50 paper-thin layers of pastry. Moroccans eat lamb often, either roasted whole or as shish kebab (bite-sized sections of skewered lamb that are barbequed over coals). Most meals are cooked in fragrant oils and garnished with spices like cumin, ginger, or pepper.

Photo by Jenny Matthews

In more traditional Moroccan homes, a woman receives a tea set on her wedding day. Moroccan tea is a mixture of green tea, a generous amount of sugar, and mint leaves. It is considered polite for a guest to drink at least three glasses of the sweet beverage.

The building blocks of old-style houses—angled into the mountainsides—are made from a mixture of earth, stones, and straw that is pressed into rectangular molds and dried in the sun.

The government has planned new housing, such as this development in Marrakech, in response to the large numbers of Moroccans who have left their rural homes to seek jobs in the cities.

Children study in a recently built village school—part of a rural development project that employed workers from the families in need of new housing, health, and educational facilities.

In contrast to the flat roofs of old mountain dwellings throughout Morocco, many of Chechaouèn's market buildings and homes feature slanted roofs finished with tile.

The great variety of Moroccan fruit—oranges, grapes, and melons, for example—offers a cooling contrast to the highly seasoned main meals. Vegetables are served at most meals and are available throughout the year. The most common of these are turnips, potatoes, and artichokes. Desserts vary from cool custards to cold, sweet pastries. Mint tea is also a part of every meal, although it is occasionally replaced by Turkish coffee. Moroccans enjoy fruit juices or water flavored with rose leaves throughout the day.

Housing

Lifestyles and economic conditions affect the housing choices of most Moroccans. In the Middle Atlas Mountains and in other remote regions, nomadic Arab and Berber families sleep in large tents, which they transport when their herds need fresh grazing land. In the High Atlas Mountains, Berber farmers have more perma-

nent dwellings. Their homes are rectangles of sun-dried bricks with roofs of straw or thatch. Such homes are often built close together and set partially into the mountainsides, with ladders connecting the lower dwellings to the higher ones. Only 2 percent of rural homes have running water, and only 4.5 percent have electricity.

Urban housing ranges from Western-style apartments and townhouses to the temporary shanties used by about 30 percent of all urban dwellers. Bidonvilles, or shantytowns, take their name from *bidon*, the French word for oil drum. Cut and flattened oil drums are the main building material of the Moroccan slums.

Many urban poor live in large residences that have been subdivided into apartments. In some cases, an entire family may live in a single room. Although the government has promised to develop low-cost housing, it has not kept pace with the large number of migrants from rural areas.

53

Courtesy of F. Botts/FAO

A Moroccan farmer uses a sickle—a curved metal blade attached to a short handle—to harvest his wheat crop.

4) The Economy

The government controls much of Morocco's economy, which remains underdeveloped. Economic activity is concentrated mostly in the cities, and great differences in income, education, and living standards exist between urban and rural areas. Morocco's per capita gross national product —the total value of goods and services produced by a country in a year—is the second lowest in North Africa.

The Moroccan working class is mostly unskilled and illiterate, and only a small number of its members (mostly in the industrial cities) are organized into unions. Unemployment in rural areas runs as high as 50 percent and in the cities may be 25 percent or more. Laws have been passed setting minimum wages, but, because workers are often unaware of their rights, urban Moroccans usually work for less.

Agriculture

Agriculture, including livestock raising, has long dominated Morocco's economy. In the early 1990s, about 50 percent of the population was employed in agriculture.

Morocco's main agricultural products are barley, wheat, vegetables, and fruit. Much of the nation's extensive fruit harvest is sold to the Soviet Union. Although once an exporter of wheat and maize (corn), Morocco now imports 2.5 million tons of wheat annually and even more maize.

54

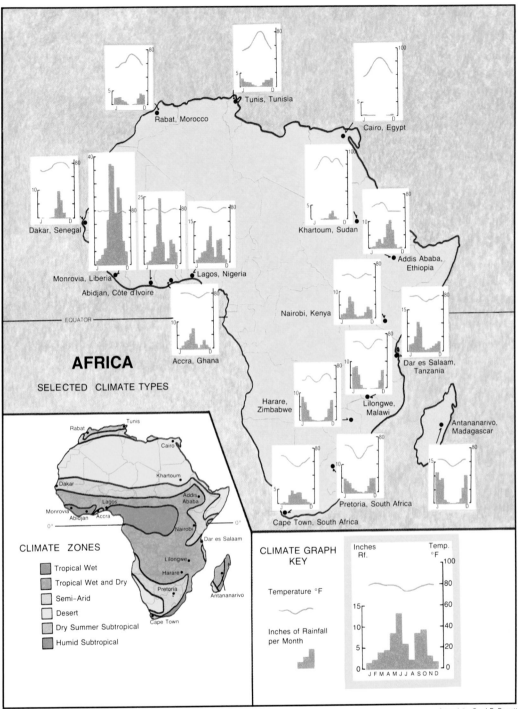

AFRICA

SELECTED CLIMATE TYPES

Rabat, Morocco

Tunis, Tunisia

Cairo, Egypt

Dakar, Senegal

Khartoum, Sudan

Addis Ababa, Ethiopia

Monrovia, Liberia

Abidjan, Côte d'Ivoire

Lagos, Nigeria

Accra, Ghana

Nairobi, Kenya

Dar es Salaam, Tanzania

Harare, Zimbabwe

Lilongwe, Malawi

Antananarivo, Madagascar

Pretoria, South Africa

Cape Town, South Africa

EQUATOR

CLIMATE ZONES

Rabat
Tunis
Cairo
Khartoum
Dakar
Addis Ababa
Lagos
Monrovia
Abidjan
Accra
Nairobi
Dar es Salaam
Lilongwe
Harare
Pretoria
Antananarivo
Cape Town
0°   0°

- Tropical Wet
- Tropical Wet and Dry
- Semi-Arid
- Desert
- Dry Summer Subtropical
- Humid Subtropical

CLIMATE GRAPH KEY

Inches
Rf.

Temp.
°F

Temperature °F

Inches of Rainfall
per Month

100
80
60
40
20
0

15
10
5
0
J F M A M J J A S O N D

Artwork by Carol F. Barrett

These climate graphs show the monthly change in the average rainfall received and in the average temperature from January to December for the capital cities of 16 African nations. Rabat, Morocco, lies on the southern edge of the Mediterranean climate zone and has relatively moist winters and dry summers. While Rabat receives a total of about 20 inches of rainfall, much of Morocco, especially to the south, is considerably drier. Data taken from *World-Climates* by Willy Rudloff, Stuttgart, 1981.

Both traditional and modern agricultural techniques are used on Morocco's farms. On the fertile Rharb Plain *(right)*, a farmer tills his field with a horse-drawn plow. Just beyond the Atlas Mountains *(below)*, extensively irrigated fields produce a zigzag pattern of different crops.

Courtesy of United Nations

Photo by Maryknoll Missioners

Two reasons for the rise in cereal imports are Morocco's growth in population and its unusual climate. Cereal products are more affected than other crops by variable moisture. If sufficient rain falls, the annual harvest produces enough to supply both local needs and export quotas. If rainfall levels are low, however, the government must import food to prevent widespread hunger. Good harvests in 1989, for example, gave Morocco an unusual agricultural surplus.

Insufficient rainfall also severely affects the goats, sheep, and cattle that graze on Morocco's farmland. In the early 1990s, Morocco had about 3.2 million cattle, 16.1 million sheep, and 5.8 million goats. In some areas, as much as 90 percent of the livestock have starved to death during droughts.

Moroccans practice two distinct types of agriculture. European settlers and a small number of wealthy Moroccan landowners use modern machinery and techniques. Small-scale landowners, on the other hand, work with wooden plows drawn by oxen. Often their tools cannot penetrate the dry earth, and their success depends on rainfall to soften the soil.

Modernization has long been the key factor in the country's plans for economic expansion. In October 1957 the government began Operation Plough to equip poorer farmers with tractor-drawn plows, fertilizers, and high-quality seeds. The government also nationalized (changed from private to government ownership) the land that France had granted to Europeans while Morocco was a protectorate. Through low-interest loans, many Moroccans bought nationalized land from the government. European farms, however, were often the most mechanized in the country, and the Moroccan farmers who took them over were unable to make the land produce as it had before.

Forestry and Fishing

The nation's forests, although potentially very valuable, remain underdeveloped because the government has yet to map them. In the early 1990s, only 10 percent of Morocco's 18.7 million acres of forest had been officially surveyed. Overgrazing and woodcutting by rural populations are also ongoing problems. Small-scale landowners—who depend on the forests for fuel-wood—and their livestock, which graze in the forests, strip about 49,000 acres of plants each year.

Morocco's most valuable trees are fir, cork oak, and cedar. Other varieties include acacia, eucalyptus, pine, thuya, and argan—a spiny evergreen that grows only in Morocco. The limited forestry industry employed roughly 65,000 people in the early 1990s. Major products include timber, cork, panels, and crates. Pulp is also produced and sold within Morocco to manufacturers of paper and cardboard.

Although the government owns all of the wooded land, it regularly grants licenses to industrial plantations and developers to harvest trees. In order to prevent erosion of the soil as forests disappear, the

A locust plague is one of the greatest threats to Morocco's food supply. Early in 1988 the nation saw the start of the worst infestation since 1954. The insects, numbering in the billions, settle on crops and other vegetation, stripping the land of plant life. At the outset of the plague, Morocco treated about 62,000 acres a day with insecticide. By 1990 the plague seemed under control.

government has begun a reforestation plan, which replants about 12,000 acres annually.

Fishing has become a major export industry in Morocco. Sardines, tuna, mackerel, and anchovies are in plentiful supply in the Atlantic waters off the western coast of Morocco. In the early 1990s, the total haul had exceeded 500,000 tons per year. Safi and Agadir are the main fishing ports, where the catch is packed and shipped to Casablanca to be treated and canned. Morocco's fish supplies were endangered in 1990, when an oil spill occurred off the country's coast.

The fish-canning industry in the early 1990s had 72 factories and an additional 100 freezing and processing plants. Although most of Morocco's fish are sent to Casablanca for processing, the government has helped to build a plant at Agadir that produces fish flour for Moroccan markets.

Manufacturing and Mining

Most of Morocco's factories are located in Casablanca and operate with foreign capital and staff. After Moroccan independence in 1956, European investors withdrew a great deal of both forms of support, creating a crisis from which Morocco is only beginning to recover. In 1990 manufacturing accounted for about 17.5 percent of the gross national product.

About 200,000 Moroccans now work in the modern industrial sector, but most manufacturing firms are small. The chemical industry is the most profitable and

Stands of cedar trees grow in one of Morocco's national parks.

A tannery worker immerses an animal hide in a tanning solution. The treated hide is then dried in the sun. Leather results from this process and is used in the manufacture of a variety of products, from camel saddles to shoes.

A colorful stack of textiles is ready for unloading at a suq.

accounts for about 33 percent of the nation's production. Textile and leather industries contribute about 15 percent of the output, while food processing supplies about 10 percent. The largest industrial employer is the textile business, with 68,000 employees.

The national government protects the textile industry with a tariff, or tax, on imports. This procedure heavily taxes incoming textiles, which makes them more expensive to buy and which allows the country's own industry to compete in the local market. Before tariffs were introduced, Moroccan textiles had attracted only 25 percent of the demand from within the country.

Mining is Morocco's main industry and is the major source of export earnings. Phosphate mining is completely owned and operated by the government. The largest phosphate deposits in the world are mined at Khouribga, near Casablanca, and at Youssoufia, east of Safi. The ports at

Suqs are a major feature of Moroccan life. Each town has its market on the same day every week.

Historically, most of Morocco's foreign trade has been with France. But Casablanca's busy port receives ships from other countries as well, among them Spain, the Soviet Union, the United States, and Saudi Arabia.

both Casablanca and Safi receive heavy international traffic, because the world purchases over 40 percent of its phosphate from Morocco.

International demand and prices for raw phosphate began to decline in the early 1980s. To compete with other suppliers, the Moroccan government has invested heavily in processing plants to turn the raw ore into finished fertilizers, which are more attractive to buyers. Four processing plants were in operation by the early

In the French-built New Town section of Fès, city life bustles with daytime traffic.

A winding road connects Rabat and Casablanca, which lie about 60 miles apart on the Atlantic coast.

1990s. Phosphate production has recently decreased because of concern over the environmental hazards of phosphate-based fertilizers.

Other important mineral deposits—including both soft and hard coals, iron, and manganese—also exist in Morocco, but these ores have not been as profitable as phosphate. World demand is not as great for coal and iron, and mining them requires expensive electrical power.

Transportation and Energy

In the early 1980s, Morocco's transportation network connected most parts of the country. Its road network now totals about 40,000 miles, but only 15,000 miles can be used in rainy weather. Main roads account for over 5,400 miles, and secondary roads extend over 4,100 miles. Most of the network lies in the plain between the Atlantic coast and the Atlas Mountains.

Traffic density in Morocco has been increasing, and in the early 1990s about 500,000 passenger cars and 247,000 commercial vehicles were registered. Regular bus service links most cities, and although small taxis must stay within city limits, larger taxis may transport passengers anywhere in the country.

Morocco has 10 ocean ports, the largest of which is in Casablanca. The country also operates 50 airports, with international runways in Casablanca, Rabat, Tangier, Marrakech, Fès, Ouarzazate, and Agadir. Royal Air Maroc, the government-owned national carrier, provides transportation for most Western tourists.

The extremely high cost of electrical power has slowed manufacturing and mining development. Morocco buys a significant amount of electrical energy from other nations, but most of its internal supply comes from 23 hydroelectric plants on rivers near Marrakech. A plant at Casablanca capable of using either anthracite (hard) coal or fuel oil has been built to provide more power.

Morocco imports oil and small amounts of coal, as well as electrical current, for its power plants in and around Rabat and

Colorful bunches of flowers for sale brighten a side street in Rabat.

Casablanca. Oil accounts for only 3 percent of Morocco's commercial energy needs, however. Coal is the country's major energy source and supplies about 54 percent of the nation's industrial needs.

Tourism

Tourism becomes more important to the Moroccan economy each year. The nation's network of hotels is extensive and well organized. Some of these accommodations are former Arab palaces that retain all of their luxury and grandeur. The roads to the principal towns are good, and visitors arrive by plane, air-conditioned train, or bus.

Winter sports on the slopes of the Atlas Mountains at Ifrane and at points farther

Among the items that vacationing shoppers will find at the markets in Fès are pottery, textiles, leather goods, metalwork, and spices.

south are very popular. The total number of visitors in the early 1990s was roughly 1.6 million, 400,000 of whom came from France. Morocco's location, climate historical sites, and beaches attract primarily Western European tourists.

The Future

Morocco's social problems have continued to intensify. As more rural workers flock to urban centers, shantytowns grow to massive size, and few people are left to work the land—once Morocco's economic mainstay. The war in the Western Sahara drained a major portion of the nation's

Bricklayers construct a home in a Moroccan village, where brickmaking materials—mud, stones, and straw—are readily available. In other rural areas, houses are built of wood and stone. Morocco's urban centers still lack sturdy, affordable housing to accommodate their growing populations.

A merchant displays a full array of fresh vegetables. Morocco's ability to provide food for its people depends on its success in fighting the locust plague as well as on its plans for modernizing farming techniques.

development budget. Food prices are subject to drastic increases, a situation made worse by crop-damaging droughts.

Hassan II, however, has initiated a number of national projects designed to cure these ills. A housing commission has begun to reward developers who produce inexpensive urban housing. A government program continues to supply more modern equipment to farmers. With this new technology, farming may again become profitable and may slow the migration of rural dwellers to the cities.

Morocco's greatest challenge, however, lies in the Western Sahara. The Polisario guerrillas—and their backers in Algeria, Mauritania, and the Soviet Union—are dedicated to self-rule by Western Saharans. Hassan II hopes the territory will choose to become a permanent part of Morocco and has agreed to a public vote among the Western Saharan people. Morocco's future, in part, depends on the outcome of that vote.

63

Index